Original title:
Starlight Stanzas

Copyright © 2025 Creative Arts Management OÜ
All rights reserved.

Author: Nathaniel Blackwood
ISBN HARDBACK: 978-1-80567-765-9
ISBN PAPERBACK: 978-1-80567-886-1

Verses Woven in Silver Threads

In the sky, a cow said, "Moo!"
Using constellations for a view.
Worms were in a dance, you see,
Beneath the moon's great comedy.

Stars winked at the odd parade,
While comets in a line just swayed.
Laughter spilled from planets bright,
As gravity struggled, lost in flight.

Seeking Solace Among the Stars

A rocket ship with squeaky wheels,
Zooms past a planet made of meals.
Cheese and crackers float on by,
As astronauts all learn to fly.

Jupiter hums a silly song,
Venus joins in, singing along.
Aliens chuckle as they spy,
Twin stars arguing in the sky.

A Heavenly Tapestry of Words

Galaxies spin with such delight,
While Saturn starts a pillow fight.
Meteor showers rain down cheer,
Tickled by laughter, can you hear?

On Mars, they toast with orange juice,
While spacetime turns into a truce.
Spaceships dance like silly fools,
In a universe that bends the rules.

Moonlit Musings and Cosmic Whispers

The moon plays peek-a-boo each night,
With squirrels wearing tiny hats, what a sight!
Galactic giggles fill the air,
As stars engage in interstellar flair.

Wishing wells float on clouds of fluff,
Where dreams come true and never bluff.
Venus slips on ice, lands with a slide,
Creating laughs on a cosmic ride.

Galactic Echoes

In the vacuum, cats float around,
Searching for treasures, bright and profound.
They chase after comets, with tails in a swirl,
In this cosmic chaos, they're queens of the world.

Stars giggle softly, playing hide and seek,
While the moon winks, cheeky and sleek.
Galaxies rumble with outrageous delight,
As aliens dance, preparing for night.

The Night Sky Speaks

When the moon starts to chuckle, oh, what a sight,
Stars burst out laughing, cozy and bright.
They swap tales of planets, each one quite odd,
One's got a disco; another's a fraud.

The Big Dipper spills coffee, what a big mess,
While Orion darts off, avoids the duress.
Planets honk horns, driving their ships,
In this cosmic carpool, stocked full of quips.

Light Trails of Thoughts

Thoughts zoom like meteors, quick on the run,
Chasing each other, oh, isn't it fun?
Ideas collide in a brilliant flash,
In the deep space of dreaming, a vibrant splash.

With one little twinkle, a giggle erupts,
As nonsense balloons in big, puffy clumps.
Thoughts loop like satellites, prancing with glee,
While cosmic chuckles bounce freely, you see?

Celestial Cadence

The stars have a rhythm, a beat of their own,
A quirky ballet, where joy brightly shone.
Planets twirl round in glittery shoes,
As constellations stomp, they jive with the blues.

Comets wear hats made of dazzling rays,
Swaying to music of heavenly plays.
With a flick and a twirl, they leap through the air,
In this cosmic circus, laughter's everywhere!

Celestial Conversations

The stars are chatting up above,
In twinkling tones and gifts of love.
They laugh at planets doing the twist,
And wink at comets that shake their fist.

A moonbeam slips on cosmic glue,
While Mars shouts, "Hey, I'm still in view!"
Saturn's rings are a disco ball,
While Venus takes a selfie—what a squall!

Jupiter's storms have a punchy flair,
And black holes swirl without a care.
A meteor dances like it's on a spree,
Shooting stars are just wishing to be free!

They prank the night with glitter and glee,
Making wishes on air, just you wait and see.
With cosmic chuckles that echo through space,
These celestial jesters put smiles on our face.

Echoes in the Dark

The moon whispers tales to the barren trees,
While stars throw confetti, riding the breeze.
A squirrel in shadows claims he's a knight,
Swinging his sword in the dead of the night.

The owl hoots jokes not fit for the meek,
While crickets chirp, "We're cool, take a peek!"
Fireflies glow with a glimmering grin,
Trying to lure all the bugs to come in.

Daredevil bats dive like they're in a race,
And raccoons play hide and seek with a face.
The night becomes lively, a whimsical scene,
Where shadows compete to steal the sheen.

Echoes of laughter ripple in the void,
A chorus of creatures, all overjoyed.
In the heart of the dark, hilarity sparks,
As nature's own jesters dance through the parks.

Stardust Dreams Entwined

A comet sneezed and off it went,
Chasing the moon with a giggly bent.
Stars play peek-a-boo, what a sight,
They twinkle and dance, oh what a night!

Aliens toss snacks from their UFOs,
Popcorn and candy, oh how it glows!
They crash for a moment on Jupiter's rack,
Then blast off again with a silly quack!

Cosmic Ballads of the Night

Singing stars strum on space guitars,
While constellations host bizarre bars.
Asteroids tap dance with meteors bold,
Telling wild tales of adventures untold.

A black hole chuckles, pulls in the light,
Stealing the glow, what a comical sight!
Saturn's rings jingle with jazzy delight,
As planets spin 'round, ready for flight!

Reflections in Midnight Waters

In the pond where fireflies chat and blink,
Frogs wear top hats, oh what do you think?
The moon takes a dip in the water's sheen,
Waves rise and laugh, it's a cosmic scene!

Stars in the sky trade their shiny flair,
While ducks in the pond spin without a care.
Ripples giggle, splashing the air,
As the echo of laughter floats everywhere!

The Enchantment of Nightly Gleams

Pixies toss sparkles with glee and cheer,
Sprinkling dreams as the night draws near.
Jesters of the cosmos prance on a beam,
Tickling the night with a luminous scheme!

Galaxies giggle in swirling delight,
While shadows play games, avoiding the light.
A moonbeam trips, lands right by my side,
Causing me to chuckle, what a wild ride!

Harmonies of the Galactic Realm

In the cosmos, there's a dance,
Aliens in a silly prance.
They trip on stars, oh what a sight,
Twinkling giggles fill the night.

Planets wobble in delight,
Jupiter's joke takes flight.
Saturn laughs with its ringed grace,
While Mars tries to keep its face.

Asteroids toss confetti beams,
Comets burst with raucous screams.
Galactic music fills the air,
With laughter floating everywhere.

So dance along the milky way,
And let the stars lead the sway.
In this realm of cosmic fun,
The jokes of space have just begun.

When Darkness Meets Twinkling Light

Oh, how the shadows prance and play,
While stars snicker at the fray.
The moon's got jokes that make us howl,
And cosmic cats that nightly prowl.

In the dark, a giggle grows,
As meteors lose all their clothes.
They streak across the velvet skies,
With laughter echoing in their flies.

The night is filled with silly dreams,
Of galaxies adorned with beams.
Comets race and trip the light,
In a madcap cosmic out of sight.

So let the night be full of cheer,
With saucy stars that come quite near.
In the dance of dark and bright,
We find our chuckles, pure delight.

Lightyears of Unspoken Verse

Across the void, a whisper flows,
Of cosmic puns that no one knows.
Aliens plot their punchlines bright,
In lightyears wrapped, a giggling sight.

Each star's a story looking to tell,
But most of them just laugh and yell.
They scribble jokes in supernova glow,
Sending giggles where no one goes.

Black holes sigh, with humor low,
As comets zip and often throw.
While planets spin with tales untold,
In this vastness, hilarity unfolds.

So strap in tight for a wacky trip,
To where the cosmic jesters skip.
In time and space, the fun's immense,
With laughter echoing in their defense.

Illuminated Hues of the Universe

In the sky, colors intertwine,
With giggles wrapped in cosmic twine.
Each hue a joke, a vibrant show,
As laughter bubbles up below.

A purple star, with one eye aglee,
Sends snickers to a yellow spree.
Green finds blue in a dance so bold,
While red just shakes, and shyly told.

The universe paints with silly glee,
With funny shapes and chaos free.
Galaxies spin in hues of jest,
A carnival where humor rests.

So let each color bring you cheer,
As the universe draws us near.
For in this vast, radiant expanse,
The funniest moments get their chance.

Radiant Reflections

In a world where stars wear hats,
They twinkle and dance, like clever cats.
One winked at me, said, 'What's your plan?'
I said, 'Just dreaming of a big pot of jam!'

The moon's a giant cheese, so bright,
What's the best topping? I think it's right.
A sprinkle of laughter, a dollop of glee,
Who knew the cosmos could cook up such spree?

The comets zoom by, with tails of flair,
Leaving behind a scent of fresh air.
They giggle and tumble, what a delight,
Making wishes on dreams, oh what a sight!

So here's to the stars, with jokes to share,
In a cosmic comedy, we're floating in air.
Let's dance with the planets, sing to the sun,
In this funny universe, we'll have lots of fun!

Nighttime Narratives

Once upon a twinkle, so bold,
A star tried to tell tales, stories untold.
But it tripped on a comet, fell on its face,
Now it giggles in corners of dark, lovely space.

The owl hoots loudly, a giggly beast,
'Who cooks the best bran muffins for feast?'
The stars nod in chorus, with light-hearted cheer,
'Only the moon, if it's not too severe!'

There's a meteor shower, with wishes galore,
One wished for socks, another for more.
As they zipped past the clouds, they swirled with delight,
Mixing up dreams in the starry night.

So let's gather 'round, hear the tales unfold,
Of cheeky little stars and their antics untold.
In the night's gentle arms, we'll laugh unconfined,
For the universe knows—funny stories unwind!

Slumbering Light

When the nighttime yawns, the stars come to play,
They take off their shoes, dance the night away.
Pajamas made of starlight, that's the style,
They twirl and they whirl in a whimsical pile.

A sleepy old sun draws a blanket of gold,
Snores so softly, its warmth is bold.
While planets tell jokes, they bounce and spin,
Making waves of laughter, let the dreaming begin!

In a quiet nook where dreams weave tight,
A sleepy star whispers, 'Is this a delight?'
With chuckles and giggles, they wrap you in light,
In this slumbering bliss, everything feels right.

So close your eyes, let the fun take its flight,
In the cuddle of darkness, all worries take flight.
For in the starlit play, where wishes ignite,
Every slumbering moment shines ever so bright!

Celestial Song

The universe sings a high-pitched tune,
From the tiniest star to the biggest balloon.
A cosmic karaoke, with echoes so funny,
Even the black holes hum—doughnut-shaped honey!

Saturn plays drums with its rings a-twirl,
While Mars strums a guitar, in a spacey whirl.
The asteroids join with a clatter and thump,
All dancing together, making quite the lump!

Through the dark expanse, laughter fills the air,
A melody brightens every cosmic affair.
As stars swirl and spin, with giggles so free,
In this celestial song, we all find our glee.

So let's sing along with the wonders beyond,
Harmonize with planets in a joyous bond.
For under this blanket of glittering night,
Every note we share shines with playful light!

Illuminated Dreams

In the night, the moonlight winks,
Cars zoom by, like shooting links.
Stars play hide and seek above,
Twinkling bright, like kittens in love.

Dreamers dance with silly glee,
Chasing thoughts like bumblebees.
A comet trips, it takes a fall,
We laugh and cheer, oh what a ball!

Galaxies spin in clumsy states,
Like sock puppets on dinner plates.
Each twinkle tells a goofy tale,
Of alien cats who chase their tail.

So let's toast to dreams tonight,
Where laughter sparkles in the light.
With each giggle, the stars beam wide,
In this cosmic circus, we all collide.

Rhythmic Starlight

Twinkling notes in the sky's parade,
The planets groove, don't be afraid.
Asteroids dance with a jolly jig,
While meteorites jump in a wig!

The Milky Way offers a stage,
Comets strut, they're all the rage.
Black holes spin like a DJ's turn,
We laugh so hard, our faces burn.

Galactic rovers roll in line,
Wobbling stars tipple like wine.
A supernova cracks a joke,
Leaving us in giggles, bespoke.

So join the party among the lights,
Where whimsy rules on starry nights.
Each beam a giggle, each flash a cheer,
Dancing with glee, the cosmos draws near.

Cosmic Composition

A symphony of silly skies,
With quirky chords that mesmerize.
Neon moons with funky flair,
Sing tunes that tickle, land and air.

The stars compose a merry song,
With melodies that feel so wrong.
Pulsars play the strings of fate,
As space cats dance, they don't hesitate.

In an orbit where jokes collide,
We spin and whirl, the universe wide.
Galactic vibes jump and sway,
Laughing til dawn in cosmic play.

So here's to tunes beyond the sphere,
Where laughter echoes – loud and clear.
With every laugh, let's make it grand,
Creating joy across this land.

The Secret Language of Stars

Whispers between the stars, we hear,
A chuckle here, a giggle near.
They share secrets with a twinkly grin,
Like gossiping friends, they pull us in.

Each wink a pun, each flash a chuckle,
Like celestial friends in a huddle.
They trade silly jokes in cosmic streams,
In this vast space of starlit dreams.

The constellations point to fun,
While space dust sparkles like freshly spun.
A nebula coughs, it's caught quite off,
While laughter breaks through, we can't help but scoff.

So gaze above, find humor bright,
In the intricate dance of the night.
For in this sky, with all its charms,
Lies a language of laughter that warms.

Starry-eyed Reflections

In the night, I see a cat,
Dancing 'neath the stars, oh what of that?
It trips on its tail, a glorious flop,
And I can't help but laugh, I just can't stop.

The moon winks at the jokes it shares,
While comets zoom with dazzling flares.
The Milky Way chuckles, what a sight!
Galactic giggles fill the night.

Asteroids roll like bowling balls,
As shooting stars dodge the cosmic halls.
A space squirrel with a twinkle so bright,
Jumps through the sparkles, what a delight!

With laughter echoing through the skies,
Constellations chuckle, no need for ties.
In this whimsical dance, I find my place,
Among cosmic jesters, I join the race.

Poetry Across the Cosmos

Zooming through space, a comet speeds,
Carrying with it all our quirky needs.
It drops off rhymes like candy bars,
While planets giggle in their twinkling cars.

Jupiter jests with its giant grin,
Each storm a punchline, where to begin?
Saturn spins jokes with its ringed flair,
While Venus chuckles, floating in air.

A cosmic poet scribbles in the dark,
Letters tumbling, igniting a spark.
On Pluto's surface, a quirky mirth,
Cosmic punchlines bring endless worth.

The stars conspire in playful glee,
Creating verses that float for free.
In this universe, laughter's the key,
Together we rhyme, you and me.

Illuminated Verses

In a realm where pixies play,
Even the rockets join the fray.
With verses bright, lighting the sky,
Sunbeams dance, they leap up high.

Galaxies giggle, twirling about,
Stars burst out in a sparkling shout.
A black hole snickers, what a cheek!
As laughing meteors start to sneak.

Nebulas bloom with colors so wild,
Space socks are lost, oh how they compiled!
Each twinkle tells a hilarious tale,
Of cosmic journeys on a shiny trail.

Laughter rolls like a comet's tail,
Joyful echoes that never pale.
In this luminous world, fun's the theme,
Join the stardust in a radiant dream.

Galactic Meditations

Close your eyes, drift away
To a universe where squirrels play.
Galactic slides and starry swings,
Laughter echoes with each small fling.

Comets wear hats that curl and twine,
Stars dressed in suits looking so fine.
Planets giggle in their spinning dance,
Inviting you to take a chance.

Asteroids juggling in a cosmic show,
While moonbeams watch and cheer below.
Galactic games of hide and seek,
In the nebulae, the sparks do peek.

With each tick of the stardust clock,
Expect delight, a cosmic shock.
In this galaxy, humor's the way,
Join the fun, come out and play.

Celestial Verses in the Dark

In the night, the stars all wink,
Like they've had too much to drink.
They giggle bright in cosmic glee,
Telling secrets to you and me.

A comet's tail, a playful swoop,
It dances like a silly loop.
The moon's a giant cheese, they say,
And mice are hoping for a play.

Meteor showers make a mess,
Like confetti, they're quite a dress.
When the sun shines, they just feel shy,
Hiding well, those stars up high.

So let's toast to the cosmic show,
With sparkly drinks, a vibrant glow.
Laughter echoes in the chill,
As starlight sparkles, sweeten this thrill.

Serenade of the Glittering Sky

In the velvet sky, they prance and twirl,
Stars giggle and spin in a giant whirl.
A shadowy planet wears a frown,
While asteroids race, flipping upside down.

Galaxies swirl like a dance-off spree,
With twinkling lights like confetti spree.
A shooting star trips on its own feet,
It gives the night a comic beat.

The moon plays hide and seek with clouds,
It peeks out, giggling, drawing crowds.
The night sky joins in a playful song,
As constellations hum along.

So let's laugh with the cosmos bright,
Dancing under the playful night.
With comets smiling, stars all tease,
The universe knows how to please.

Nightfall's Poetic Glow

When the sun takes its final bow,
The stars laugh, "Look at us now!"
They gather round for a glittery feast,
Complaining of light like a noisy beast.

A slumbering world under a twinkling sky,
Stars poke fun at the sleeping guy.
"Hey, Earth, we're the ones in charge,
We'll light the night; let's have a charge!"

Planets wobble in a silly dance,
While comets laugh at their own chance.
With each flicker, there's a punchline tossed,
The stars proclaim, "You can't be lost!"

So let's ride the moonbeam slide,
Where all the giggles and sparkles collide.
With nocturnal humor in the air,
The universe sings without a care.

Constellation Chronicles

In a sky with a million pranks,
Constellations join in merry ranks.
They draw figures, of cows and dogs,
While giggling like silly frogs.

The Big Dipper spills its moonlit tea,
As little stars shout, "Hey, look at me!"
Orion flexes with dramatic flair,
But a meteor shower gives him a scare.

The northern lights play peek-a-boo,
While Saturn winks in rings of glue.
"Oh, this is just cosmic ballet,"
They laugh at clumsy Milky Way.

So let's sit back, enjoy the view,
Watch the antics, see what they do.
As the universe spins in timeless jest,
Stars remind us to laugh the best.

Cosmic Soliloquy

In the cosmos where cows float,
A rocket ship rides a soap bubble coat.
Aliens play chess with green frogs,
While comets chase after lazy dogs.

Planets spin in ballet of glee,
As stars wink at the moon's old marquee.
A supernova had quite the bling,
But lost it all in a dance-off fling.

Galaxies twirl like they're at a feast,
While black holes giggle, not bothered in the least.
Asteroids throw a glittery bash,
With confetti made from stardust and ash.

So come join this cosmic chuckle and cheer,
Where the universe spins in a groove so dear.
With cosmic jokes that tickle your soul,
Each laugh is a shooting star on a roll.

Twilight's Embrace

Night descends on a pogo stick,
Jumping over buildings, oh what a trick!
The sun takes a bow with a grand old grin,
While shadows skedaddle, trying to win.

A bat wore sunglasses, feeling too cool,
Sipping on nectar from a luminous pool.
Fireflies giggle, lighting paths with flair,
While owls do the cha-cha, without a care.

Clouds become pillows in this twilight hour,
As giraffes dance salsa beneath a star shower.
Balloons float past with a giggly squeak,
And stars take selfies, feeling quite chic.

So let twilight wrap you in laughter and light,
Where every silly moment feels just right.
In this wacky soirée, let your heart race,
For life in the stars is a marvelous place!

Dreaming Among the Stars

Wishing on stars with a wink and a grin,
A cat in a rocket, about to begin.
With marshmallow clouds and jellybean dreams,
The universe giggles, or so it seems.

Shooting stars race on roller coasters high,
While giggling comets zoom past the sky.
A fluffy unicorn sips starlit tea,
While space fish bubble, quite happily.

Rockets get stuck in galactic traffic,
As aliens dance, feeling quite dramatic.
Meteors play hopscotch in cosmic schools,
While planets exchange their shiny jewels.

So let us dream in this whimsical space,
Where laughter and wonder fill every place.
Among the stars, let your spirit soar,
In dreams that are funny, forevermore!

Whispers of the Universe

The universe whispers with a chuckle and cheer,
Tickling the planets that orbit so near.
Aliens giggle in spacesuits so bright,
Playing hopscotch with gravity, full of delight.

The Milky Way's a twisty slide,
Where meteors race and comets glide.
Black holes hold secrets, spinning tales,
Of interstellar pirates with glittery sails.

Stars share jokes in a shimmering haze,
While planets do the moonwalk in playful ways.
Quantum quokkas wiggle with glee,
As cosmic dust sprinkles tea for tea.

So listen closely to the cosmic tune,
Where laughter echoes from sun to moon.
With every whisper, find joy in the quirk,
For the universe dances with a smirk!

Whispering Galaxies

In a nearby galaxy, a cat did meow,
Wishing on planets, 'Where's my fun meow?'
Stars chuckled softly, twinkling with glee,
'Hold on there, furball, just wait and see!'

Aliens danced with their antennas high,
Practicing moves under a purple sky.
One slipped on stardust, oh what a sight,
'Tripping on space? Now that's pure delight!'

Laughter erupted from comets that raced,
Chasing their tails in a cosmic embrace.
Galactic giggles floated through the air,
As squirrels in space played tag without care.

The Dance of Light

A firefly waltzed in the silvery breeze,
Dodging moonbeams as it danced with ease.
'Is this a party?' it asked with a grin,
'Hope there's enough for all of us in!'

The sunbeams joined, flashing like confetti,
Twinkling in rhythm, oh so unsteady.
A disco ball formed from a heavy star,
And the planets rocked it, they shone from afar.

'Put on your shoes!' shouted a bright comet,
'Let's boogie down, don't you dare forget!'
Soon the night air was filled with laughter,
As they spun and twirled, happily ever after.

Vesper Verses

The fireflies scribbled on twilight's page,
Writing their secrets in light, so sage.
'There's wisdom in bugs!' a beetle proclaimed,
'Take notes, fellow critters, let's get this named!'

A cricket piped up, 'Now don't be absurd,
Who cares about wisdom? Let's dance, spread the word!'
With a flick of its wings, a party ignited,
As laughter erupted from all those invited.

Each verse of the evening rang out with joy,
Creating a chorus that none could destroy.
When darkness embraced, the whimsy just grew,
Under the blanket of a heavenly hue.

Nightfall Rhapsody

When twilight arrived with a wink and a tease,
The stars all gathered, begging for cheese.
A rabbit in space sang a tune so bright,
'Let's feast on the moon, it tastes just right!'

The owls hooted softly, asking for more,
While the milky way wobbled, knocking on the door.
'Who's ordering pizza?' a star called aloud,
'The heavens are hungry, let's feast on a cloud!'

Laughter erupted across the night sky,
As the sun peeked in, with a curious eye.
'Take your nightcap and share in the fun,
For dawn will be here, but let's dance till we're done!'

Nebula Narratives

In a vacuum, the socks vanishing,
Aliens dance, while I'm just banishing.
Stars twinkle like a shiny prize,
While comets race to make me rise.

Galaxies spin in a whirl of cheer,
Cosmic jokes told from far and near.
Planets trip on their own two feet,
In space, who knew? It's such a treat!

Meteor showers; who can catch?
Shooting stars? I just found a match.
With each wish, a giggle flies,
As the universe throws its pie in the skies.

Black holes quietly munching a snack,
Spinning tales while the whole world's black.
I cheer for the stars, for making my day,
In their comedic dance, I'm swept away.

Cosmic Rhythms

Saturn's rings play a funky beat,
While asteroids groove, oh, so sweet.
A moonwalk here, a space hop there,
Alien jokes float through the air.

Venus flips with a wink and grin,
Jupiter laughs as they all spin.
Galactic pranks in the heavenly night,
Stars burp and giggle, what a sight!

Twinkling lights have a party in the sky,
While I'm below, attempting to fly.
In the radius of cosmic cheer,
The universe whispers, "Never fear!"

Constellations that form silly shapes,
Drawing giggles from the starscape.
Astrobiologists giggle in glee,
For the stars' funny ways are plain to see!

A Symphony of Stars

In the concert hall of the darkened night,
Stars strum their strings with sheer delight.
A galaxy's chorus, with laughs and tunes,
Sings silly tales of the man on the moons.

Planets sway in a funny little jig,
While black holes spin—the ultimate gig.
Shooting stars harmonize, a twinkling song,
Through the universe where we all belong.

Oh, the great big cosmos conducts the show,
with starry musicians stealing the glow.
Laughter echoes through infinite space,
As cosmic giggles dance and race.

Even supernovas burst in pure joy,
Filling the void with a bright little ploy.
So next time you gaze at the night's sweet charms,
Remember the jokes in the universe's arms!

Celestial Dreams

Whispers of stars flicker with cheer,
As I drift off, the cosmos draws near.
In dreams where galaxies play hide and seek,
Laughter erupts, and the universe speaks.

Comet tails swirl like candy floss,
While space cats dance, a frolicsome boss.
Bouncing on meteors, they leap with glee,
In celestial dreams, I'm utterly free.

Nibbling on stardust, what a treat,
In a moonbeam café, snacks can't be beat.
Planets break into curious song,
As they all strut about to the cosmic throng!

In this realm where giggles ignite,
I twirl with comets, wrapped in starlight.
So dream on, dear friend, let your smile beam,
In a universe bright with the wildest dream!

Twilight Musings

Under the moon, the frogs do croon,
Bouncing along like a raucous tune.
Stars in the sky, they're winking away,
While squirrels play cards, what a silly display.

Clouds drift by, making quirky shapes,
A giraffe in a bowtie, escaping from apes.
The night is alive with a giggling breeze,
As cats on a rooftop charm all the trees.

So grab a snack, don't fret about fate,
The cosmos is laughing, it's never too late.
With each twinkling star, a joke is revealed,
A universe full of fun, and it's all unconcealed.

Let's dance with the comets, sing to the light,
In this goofy dreamland, everything's right.
The cosmos is quirky, it joins in our fun,
Chasing the laughter till the night is done.

Starlit Stories

Beneath the glow, we spin a tale,
Of cheeky raccoons who set sail.
With a treasure map made of cookie crumbs,
They search for gold while the humor hums.

A gnome in a hat, just short of a height,
Tries juggling stars, what a comical sight!
With wobbly feet, he dances around,
Till he trips on a comet and smacks on the ground.

The owls throw a party in the old oak tree,
With dancing and hooting, oh what glee!
Their disco ball twinkles, shining so bright,
As fireflies join in and light up the night.

So listen closely to the tales that unfold,
Of critters and stars, with laughter retold.
Every flicker above holds a whimsy, a cheer,
In this charming nightscape, the fun is sincere.

Cosmic Cadence

A meteor showers down with style,
While aliens bicker over their cosmic dial.
"Did you press the button?!" one insists with a shout,
"Now we're lost in a black hole with no way out!"

Jupiter's moons throw a dance-off tonight,
Twisting and turning in sheer delight.
While Saturn's rings spin a wild twist,
Grumpy old Mars just shakes his fist.

On the Milky Way, there's a conga line,
Dancing with stars, oh what a sight divine!
The rhythm is catchy, it makes you want to sway,
Even black holes can't suck this groove away!

In this endless ballet of laughter and cheer,
All beings unite, the fun's always near.
Cosmic shenanigans make the night bright,
As we jive with the universe, giggling in flight.

The Universe in Rhyme

In a galaxy far, whispers of fun,
Silly spaceships race; they're second to none.
With rocket boosters painted in bright hues,
Chasing each other, they dodge the stars' blues.

Asteroids play tag, zooming near and far,
While clever meteors compete in a car.
It's a race to the finish amidst giggles and cheers,
With the lights of the cosmos applauding their gears.

A star falls down; it wishes for cake,
While Saturn's rings giggle, "Let's have a bake!"
Planets gather 'round, bringing sweets from their homes,
As they feast on their joy in delightful blooms.

So celebrate this night with laughter so wide,
The universe sings and dances with pride.
For in every twinkle, a chuckle, a rhyme,
In this grand tapestry, we all find our time.

Aurora's Silent Rhapsody

In the sky, colors dance bright,
Twirling around with pure delight.
A moose in shades of pink does prance,
While stars shake hands in a silly dance.

A penguin wearing a top hat bold,
Winks at the sun, so clever and cold.
While owls in pajamas hoot and cheers,
Laughing at whispers no one else hears.

Celestial Whispers

Comets sing like a rusty tune,
Balloons float up to greet the moon.
The clouds wear socks all mismatched,
While cheeky stars play games they've hatched.

A cat with wings says, "Look at me!"
While space ants join a grand tea spree.
Cosmic giggles bounce around,
In this jolly vast playground.

Echoes of the Night Sky

Planets roll like bowling balls,
As meteors run through cosmic halls.
A bear on a rocket takes a ride,
While laughter echoes, full of pride.

The moon steals cheese from a bright sun,
A chase ensues, it's all in fun!
Wily raccoons in capes take flight,
Dancing through this silly night.

Moonlit Verses

Bunnies hop with starry hats,
Kicking it with the funky rats.
A turtle sings the blues on high,
Marking time as the fireflies fly.

Chickens play cards up in the sky,
Cackling jokes that make you cry.
While fish in space swim along,
Chanting out a cosmic song.

Whispers of the Celestial Night

In the dark, the stars giggle,
They twinkle like they've cracked a riddle.
A comet zooms by, yelling 'Hey!',
While planets dance, come out and play!

A meteor shower, what a sight,
Let's catch wishes, oh so light!
A moonbeam slips on cosmic ice,
And trips, but hey, that's just nice!

Luminous Echoes Beneath the Moon

The moon wears shades, it's quite bizarre,
It thinks it's the brightest star.
Stars wink back, rolling their eyes,
As aliens giggle in crazy disguise.

A rocket lands near a tree,
Squirrels in helmets shout with glee!
They toast with acorns to the night,
Celebrating their goofy flight.

Chasing Dreams in Twilight's Embrace

Chasing fireflies through the dusk,
They tease us like a cosmic musk.
Twilight whispers silly things,
As shadows play with invisible strings.

A troll on a cloud sings 'La la la!',
Forgetting he's lost in a giant jar.
We laugh as we chase, hopping in glee,
Dancing with dreams as wild as can be!

Radiance of Distant Worlds

From a planet of jelly and goo,
Comes a dance party, bright and true.
Squishy beings wear hats made of light,
Bouncing around, what a silly sight!

Galaxies giggle with stellar delight,
As space ducks swim in neon light.
Each star has a tale, each glow a jest,
In this cosmic circus, we're all so blessed!

The Language of the Night

The moon speaks in giggles, oh so bright,
While stars tell jokes that take flight.
Comets pass by with a wink,
Whispering secrets we barely think.

A shadow laughs, hiding in the trees,
Tickling fireflies, buzzing with glee.
The owls hoot punchlines, so absurd,
As crickets chirp, spreading the word.

Nighttime strokes its silly chin,
Dancing shadows, where fun begins.
The sky is a canvas, laughter paints,
In the verse of night, every star faints.

So let's join this whimsical show,
Beneath the sparkling like a cosmic glow.
Let laughter echo in the night,
As dreams take flight, pure delight.

Ethereal Ballads

In the air, a giggle floats near,
Notes of the night, light as a deer.
The stars sway, talking silly dreams,
While the universe giggles at all our schemes.

The planets join in, a cheerful band,
Playing music from another land.
Saturn spins with a hula-hoop,
While Jupiter forms a dance crew's loop.

Venus chirps puns with a wink,
As meteors tumble, quick as a blink.
A melody of laughter fills the sky,
As constellations wink and sigh.

In this cosmic party, all are free,
To laugh, to dance, to just be me.
With ethereal ballads, we sing along,
To the night's funny, whimsical song.

Dreamscapes of the Cosmos

In the cosmos, dreams are quite bizarre,
Where cupcakes float and clouds are cars.
Galaxies spin like tops in play,
Painting the night in a funny way.

Nebula giggles, hiding shyly,
As stars burst forth, saying hi-y-ly!
A black hole cracks a cosmic joke,
While asteroids dance in a clumsy cloak.

Objects wander, all with flair,
Wobbling comets fly through the air.
Dreamscapes twist, they prance and gleam,
A theatrical night, or so it seems.

So hop on a star, and let's explore,
The humor of space, we can't ignore.
In the cosmos' embrace, we twirl so bright,
Lost in giggles, under moonlight.

Secrets of the Milky Way

The Milky Way whispers, shh, just here,
A secret club of laughter and cheer.
Stars share tales that make us grin,
While black holes tease and pull us in.

The dust of ages sparkles like gold,
With funny stories just waiting to be told.
Comets ink scripts of silly dreams,
As galaxies chuckle, bursting at the seams.

Nebulas dance in swirling delight,
Twirling around in the depths of night.
Memories of stars echo in tune,
Filling the air with a comic boon.

So come gather 'round, let's laugh and play,
In the secrets of the Milky Way.
With every twinkle, a joke takes flight,
In the arms of darkness, we find our light.

Constellation Revelations

In the sky, a cow jumps high,
While chickens dance, oh me, oh my!
Orion forgot where his pants went,
And now he's looking quite bent.

Taurus thinks he's quite a star,
But he can't find his nearest bar.
The Big Dipper's full of soup,
Serving stars in a cosmic loop.

Pisces swims with careless flair,
Wearing glitter in his hair.
They argue where the moonlight's been,
Stealing glimpses at the din.

As comets blaze through night's embrace,
They play tag in the velvet space.
The galaxy giggles in delight,
As planets twirl in a starry night.

Dreams Beneath the Stars

In a field where nightflowers sway,
I dreamed about a cat ballet.
They pirouetted under the moon,
While cows hummed a silly tune.

A dog dressed up as a space cat,
He said, "The cheese falls just like that!"
And aliens asked for a dance,
In their shiny new spaceship pants.

Bunnies hopped to a beat so sweet,
In cosmic socks upon their feet.
We sipped juice made from moonbeams bright,
Frolicking till the dawn's first light.

Then we woke and found it was day,
With sunlit wishes led astray.
Yet in dreams, the fun never ends,
In galaxies where laughter bends.

Luminous Lines

Across the cosmic canvas wide,
Scribbly stars take poetic pride.
One giggles, "I'm plain out of ink!"
Another replies, "Just blink, then think!"

A comet flies to find his rhyme,
While wishes giggle, wasting time.
The sun decided to paint some cheer,
And the moon just rolled his eyes in fear.

Each twinkle tells a quirky joke,
Like when Jupiter fell for a bloke.
He tripped on a meteorite's tail,
And laughed as he started to sail!

Even Saturn's rings chime in glee,
As they spin cups of cosmic tea.
So grab a quill and jot it down,
For stars want to wear your crown!

Galaxy of Words

In the deep of space, they form a group,
Words twirling, like a cosmic loop.
With laughter echoing through the void,
The puns of Pluto left us overjoyed.

"Venus wants to sing a song,
But her pitch is totally wrong!"
Mars cracks jokes about his red blush,
While Earth just rolls, "Oh! What a rush!"

"Throughout the cosmos, let's unite,
And write a tale that feels just right."
"Let's rhyme our woes and cosmic dreams,
While sipping coffee from starry streams."

As comets raced and meteors fell,
Galaxy giggles spread quite well.
The night has whispers full of fun,
In this wordy world, we've just begun!

The Light Between Us

In the night, we dance and sway,
Our shadows play in a silly way.
With twinkling stars and a wink so bright,
We giggle at the bumps in flight.

Comets zoom as we share our snacks,
Space treats giving us cosmic whacks.
I tripped on stardust, you held me tight,
Both laughing till we saw the light.

Moonbeam laughter fills the air,
With playful wishes everywhere.
We make up jokes about the sun,
In the cosmic chuckles, we have fun.

So grab your starry hat and join,
In this cosmic dance, let's not disappoint.
The universe winks, it knows our game,
In the light between us, there's no shame.

Astral Reflections

Reflective beams in a silver haze,
We gossip under the Milky Way's gaze.
Echoes of laughter fill the void,
As we poke at planets like they're toys.

Giggles bounce from star to star,
Our jokes travel wide, oh how far!
Black holes absorb the punchlines' fate,
While meteors dash, we celebrate.

Floating dreams in a cosmic stew,
We share silly tales and make them new.
With each bright twinkle, we toast the night,
Wishing on wishes that feel just right.

So here's to the humor found on high,
In the astral realms, let laughter fly.
With every twinkling joke we share,
We paint the universe with fun and flair.

Poems of the Cosmic Veil

Behind the veil where the cosmos sings,
We fashion laughter from ephemeral wings.
Stars whisper secrets, oh what a thrill,
Tickling our fancies with cosmic will.

Galaxies twirl in a dance so mad,
As we joke about the things we've had.
Supernova pranks spark joy in flight,
Lighting up the canvases of night.

Stardust spills from our giggling mouths,
As we chart the paths of celestial routes.
With a wink and a nudge, we jest at time,
In this cosmic play, our hearts will rhyme.

So pen your laughs on the astral scroll,
In the cosmic veil, we find our whole.
Each rhyme a star, each pun a light,
In this galactic joke, everything's bright.

Celestial Melodies at Dusk

As the day dims to a perfect hum,
We chase the stars, our laughter a drum.
With melodies rich as the twilight hue,
Our quirky thoughts set the sky askew.

Fireflies float with a flicker and glow,
While we compose a comical show.
The sun winks down, a cheeky goodbye,
As we throw confetti to the sky.

The clouds giggle as they drift about,
In our cosmos, there's no room for doubt.
With twirling planets, we laugh aloud,
Creating joy that's wildly unbowed.

So join the fun as the dusk unfolds,
In celestial melodies, our laughter holds.
With every giggle, every note we share,
In this cosmic symphony, we declare!

The Poetry of Silence

In a world where whispers play,
The mouse outsmarts the cat each day.
In my coffee cup, I hear a shout,
And all my worries fade out loud.

With socks that never find their pairs,
I laugh at life and all its snares.
A secret dance upon the floor,
The dust bunnies know what's in store.

So here I sit with shoes untied,
The cat and I, we share our pride.
We'll draft a scheme to catch that bird,
In moments scrawled, unheard, absurd.

And when the moon begins to rise,
I'll wear my pants with mismatched dyes.
With laughter echoing through the night,
In silence, we'll find pure delight.

Lunar Lines

The moon grins wide, a cheese delight,
It handmade jokes to share at night.
A dancing star began to twirl,
And fell right down to greet the girl.

A comet zipped by, with shoes on fire,
"Catch me if you can!" it did conspire.
Planets snickered at their fate,
While asteroids plotted a prank so great.

Galaxies twinkled in their own way,
Making faces that simply sway.
I chuckled loud, they winked in glee,
What cosmic jesters they could be!

As dreams drift high through velvet skies,
I'll ponder all their clever lies.
A chorus sings from space so wide,
On laughter's wings, our hearts abide.

Celestial Reverie

In realms where planets paint the skies,
A funky dance that mystifies.
A star with shades took flight today,
And slipped right through, but laughed, "Okay!"

Asteroids rolled like bowling balls,
While meteors wrote on cosmic walls.
A rocket ship with pops and fizz,
Declared, "The universe is ours, that's whiz!"

On Saturn's rings, I found my hat,
The universe chuckled at that!
I'm a space explorer with a flair,
Caught in a riddle, floating in air.

And as I drift on silvery streams,
The cosmos twirls in funny dreams.
A galactic laugh at life's parade,
In starlit joy, our fears all fade.

Songs of the Night

The owl hoots a quirky tune,
While crickets dance beneath the moon.
A raccoon sings with such delight,
Our nightly jam, a silly sight!

The shadows sway as laughter blooms,
A choir formed of nighttime glooms.
They cackle and giggle, what a view,
Beneath the stars, they know just what to do.

With fireflies flashing, disco lights,
They cast their glow on playful sights.
The stars above join in the song,
Reminding us that here we belong.

So let's embrace this laughter spree,
In moonlit folly, wild and free.
As night unfolds its joyful charms,
We sway together, safe in arms.

Enchanted Nightscape

The moon wore a grin, quite like a jest,
A raccoon on the roof, feeling the best.
Stars giggled out loud, twinkling with cheer,
While marzipan clouds swirled, bringing good beer.

Fireflies did the cha-cha, dancing with flair,
A comet flew by, waving with a stare.
The owl cracked a joke, all the night critters laughed,
Even the cat, who was busy with craft.

Suddenly a shadow, who could it be?
A hedgehog was waltzing, oh so carefree!
With a wink and a smile, he borrowed the show,
While the nighttime parade put on quite a glow.

With laughter and joy, the stars fell in line,
Each painting their wishes, as bright as wine.
In this enchanted night, with mischief and fun,
The world felt alive, under antics undone.

Celestial Mosaic

In the sky's vast canvas, colors collide,
A purple elephant wearing a ride.
Stars hummed a tune, vibrant and spry,
As ticklish comets flew, oh so high!

A jester sat jesting upon a star's hat,
While Venus played chess with a friendly cat.
Galaxies twirled in a cosmic conga,
And planets brought snacks, oh, what a saga!

The sun took a nap, wrapped up in sunbeams,
Dreaming of doughnuts, or so it seems.
A moonbeam reported, "Time for a prank!"
And Jupiter laughed, giving Mars a yank.

As laughter echoed through the nebula thick,
The universe chuckled, with every little trick.
In this mosaic of fun, each twinkle's a song,
Celestial mischief, where all feel they belong.

Aurora of Emotions

Dancing lights played tag in the frosty cold,
Tickling each star with stories bold.
A grumpy old star fell down to his knees,
And begged the bright colors to brighten his tease.

"Dear pink and green waves, come lend me your cheer,
For I've lost my sparkle, or so it appears."
The colors all giggled, with radiant flair,
As they painted his cheeks and combed out his hair.

With every blush, the night swirled anew,
The auroras chuckled, in vibrant hue.
They twisted and turned, like a merry go round,
While the cosmos threw confetti all over the ground.

From giggles to bubbles, the frosty night sang,
And even the moons joined in on the clang.
In an aurora of giggles, emotions would sway,
For nothing's quite dull when the colors display.

Celestial Poetry

Words spun like cotton candy in the night,
As asteroids stumbled, trying to take flight.
The universe whispered in verses so sweet,
Even black holes twirled, in a cosmic beat.

A poet sat writing on a shooting star,
With lines that flew further than he could by car.
Through metaphors wild, and similes bright,
Each stanza was sprinkled with giggles and light.

A dragonfly swooped, pen poised in its claws,
Jotting down stories of celestial laws.
"Why can't ducks fly?" it scribbled in jest,
While the sun blinked twice, enjoying the quest.

As words twinkled softly, like laughter from birth,
Cosmic poetry bloomed, giving joy to the earth.
In these verses of fun, where whimsy takes hold,
Each line sparkles bright, like treasures of old.

Orbital Echoes

Planets in party clothes, they dance,
With moons doing a silly prance.
Asteroids juggling, what a sight,
Galaxies giggle, oh what delight!

Stars swap jokes across the sky,
Halting space traffic, oh my, oh my!
A comet sneezes, it leaves a trail,
Space laughs so hard, it starts to wail.

Black holes pull in the punchlines,
While meteors twirl on cosmic vines.
Gravity's just a playful tease,
Falling for laughter, did you see?

In this universe, humor's the key,
Where stardust smiles, and so do we.
Eclipses hide giggles, shy as can be,
But when they return, it's a cosmic spree!

Twinkling Thoughts

In a galaxy far, far away,
Stars tell tales at the end of the day.
With bright-eyed smiles and cheeky grins,
They plot amusing cosmic sins.

One star says, "I'm feeling shy,"
"Hide me in a meteor's eye!"
Another chimes in, "Oh what glee,
Let's all wear hats like we're at tea!"

The sun winks, with a golden ray,
"Lighten up, it's my birthday today!"
The moon joins in, with a playful sigh,
"Bring on the cake—I'm too full, oh my!"

Galactic pranks in rhythm flow,
As comets chase with a giggly glow.
Twinkling thoughts on cosmic paths,
Bring laughter amid the universe's math!

Ethereal Poetry

Floating verses in the breeze,
Cosmic rhymes that aim to please.
A nebula hums a tune so bright,
While stars recite beneath the night.

With planets swirling in a jig,
They dance around on a cosmic twig.
Poetry drips from the heavens high,
As laughter wobbles across the sky.

The cosmos scribbles with silly haste,
Creating humor with each little taste.
Galaxies spin with wit galore,
Chasing laughs that forever soar.

Oh, the wonders that the void can bring,
In this realm where the stardust sings.
Ethereal poetry, pure and true,
Is nothing but fun, just for you!

Chasing the Comets

Chasing comets, what a thrill,
With rocket boots, we zoom and spill.
Dodging space debris, funny scenes,
They wave their tails like happy machines.

A comet trips, what a disaster,
Leaving behind a cosmic plaster.
The stars all chuckle, "What a flight!"
As we dance in laughter through the night.

With our helmets on, we're all set,
To catch the jokes we won't forget.
Supernovas pop with cheer and shine,
In this strange world, humor's divine.

So hold on tight and don't let go,
Join the chase, let giggles flow.
As we laugh through the cosmos' charms,
Wrapped in laughter, safe in our arms!

Harmonics of the Heavens

In the night, the stars do sing,
A chorus led by a cosmic king.
They twinkle like a disco ball,
Doing the moonwalk, oh what a haul!

Jupiter's got a gassy grin,
While comets dance, and round they spin.
Neptune's blue, a giant pool,
Splashing about, it's pretty cool!

Asteroids giggle as they zoom,
Trying to find a cosmic room.
But all they find is space and dust,
In their celestial wanderlust!

So gather 'round and take a peek,
The universe is far from bleak.
With laughter echoes through the night,
The heavens play, a joyful sight!

Glittering Paradigms

Stars parade in shiny hats,
Debating where the moonlight chats.
Mars throws confetti in the air,
While Venus spins like she don't care!

Galaxies swirl like cotton candy,
Making sweets that look quite dandy.
Black holes hide, but we know they play,
Pretending to be shy all day.

Shooting stars take selfies fast,
Pouting, 'Will this moment last?'
With filters made of cosmic rays,
They capture and post their starry gaze!

Join the fun in the stellar night,
Where every giggle is cosmic light.
In the dance of the universe, no doubt,
It's a party we can't live without!

Reflections in the Night

The moon peeks out with a cheeky wink,
While stars spark up with a glittering blink.
The Milky Way spills jokes from afar,
Shooting giggles like a playful star!

A telescope whispers, 'Look at that!'
As a comet trips over its own spat.
Planets flip-flop, then tumble around,
In a cosmic circus, laughter abound!

Astro-kittens play with the sun,
Chasing rays, oh what fun!
Even the black holes try to keep pace,
Grinning wide in the vast open space.

So laugh with me under this night,
With sky and stars, a frolicking sight.
In cosmic secrets, joy takes flight,
Reflecting humor in soft moonlight!

Cosmic Enchantments

Pluto pouts, it's feeling small,
While the sun throws a great big ball.
Crazy orbits, a dizzy dance,
Even the asteroids take a chance!

Saturn's rings like hula hoops,
With all the planets doing loops.
Uranus laughs at gravity's pull,
Spinning tricks, oh isn't it cool?

Nebulas fluff like cotton pillows,
Hosting starry, floaty fellows.
Supernovae burst with a roar,
Exploding laughter forever more!

So let's spin tales of celestial cheer,
Where the universe whispers in your ear.
In cosmic charms, we'll twinkle and shine,
With giggles and stardust, it's all divine!

Astral Imprints

In the night sky, a cow flips,
With a moonlit smile, taking trips.
Stars giggle, in shiny clothes,
As comets bump their silly nose.

Aliens dance with a quirky style,
Trading jokes with a cosmic smile.
Planets wobble, high as a kite,
Saying silly things 'til the morning light.

Galaxies spin like a child at play,
Drawing doodles in a starry ballet.
Everyone's laughing, all around,
In this universe, joy is found.

So if you glimpse a star that winks,
Know it chuckles, and it thinks.
That every twinkle in the sky,
Hides a joke that'll make you sigh!

Nocturnal Ink

The night is penned with a quirky twist,
As owls scribble in a dark mist.
Bats write letters, upside down,
While the moon dons a silly crown.

Frogs croak poems, in a neat parade,
All the critters join in charade.
A spider spins webs of witty lines,
Caught in laughter, a world that shines.

Shooting stars make wishes for fun,
Casting jokes as they swiftly run.
Each ripple in the pond will quack,
As the night takes a joyride back.

When dawn awakens the scribble spree,
It'll chuckle soft, just wait and see.
Because even ink, under starry gleam,
Knows how to pen a funny dream!

Lightyear Lyrics

In the galaxy, a tune takes flight,
A melody draped in cosmic light.
Aliens giggle with rhymes so bright,
Creating jokes that take the night.

Asteroids bounce, with laughter pure,
Their rocky paths, a dance demure.
Zany verses float like a cloud,
Booming laughter, oh so loud!

The sun strums a silly guitar,
While planets twirl just like a star.
Space cats sing, with a meow and cheer,
In this concert, there's naught to fear.

So grab your friends, don't miss the beat,
Join this cosmic, funny retreat.
For in the depths of the universe vast,
Laughter's a tune that forever lasts!

Starstruck Serenades

Under the stars, a clown takes stage,
Wearing a hat, full of cosmic cage.
He juggles moons and rings of dust,
Tickling the night with stardust rust.

A quirky comet, with a name like Boop,
Swings by singing in a silly loop.
Planets giggle, they sway in time,
Rhythm of laughter, a spacey rhyme.

Galactic jesters toss out lines,
Tickling the void, where humor shines.
Even the sun can't hide its grin,
For jokes like these, we all must win!

As dusk unravels its velvet shawl,
Join in the laughter, the cosmic call.
With every twinkle, an echo's play,
Starstruck giggles, forever stay!

Lost in a Celestial Sea

Floating on a starry wave,
I waved at a comet, oh so brave.
It winked back; what a sight,
A cosmic dance of pure delight.

Jellyfish in space, I swear!
They waved their tentacles, with flair.
I tried to catch a falling star,
But ended up stuck in my car.

Asteroids zoom like racecars fly,
I cheered for my favorite guy.
But then I missed my turn to Mars,
I think my GPS's got scars.

In this ocean, I found some fun,
The Milky Way's the best run!
With aliens grinning ear to ear,
They laughed at my half-hearted cheer.

Sounds of the Night Sky

Whispers of the moonlit night,
Crickets chirp, a comedic sight.
The stars chuckle at my plight,
As I trip on my own two feet tight.

A shooting star sings off-key,
While I'm trying to sip my tea.
The universe's jukebox, unmatched,
Plays songs of old, slightly scratched.

I hear the galaxy snicker loud,
As I dance like a goofy cloud.
A meteor grins, then turns to flee,
Afraid of my two left feet spree.

The echoes of the cosmos play,
In rhythms that make me sway.
Laughter bubbles from afar,
I groove, not knowing where we are.

An Affair with the Cosmos

I met a planet with a pout,
Gave me a wink, I gave a shout.
It whispered tales of love and gloom,
As I swirled in its cosmic room.

Asteroids crashed a party near,
With snacks made of stardust beer.
I danced with Saturn, what a spin,
Though it's tough with all those rings to pin.

Venus tossed me a bouquet,
But I sneezed; it floated away.
The universe chuckled at my fate,
As I moonwalked, but not quite straight.

In this love fest, there's no good byes,
Just laughter under candy skies.
Together we twirl, twinkle, and tease,
It's an affair that aims to please.

The Language of Stars

Stars gossip in twinkling tones,
About Earthlings and their funny phones.
They giggle at our midnight snacks,
And how we sometimes wear mismatched slacks.

Planets play tag, a cosmic race,
While I just try to keep up the pace.
With orbiting jokes that fly so high,
I chuckle as I give it a try.

Constellations draw a sketch of fate,
But it feels like I'm consistently late.
They point and laugh at my mishap,
As I trip on gravity's constant trap.

The universe speaks in humorous ways,
Filling our nights with laugh-filled rays.
So let's twirl and giggle till dawn,
For in this vast space, we carry on.

Glimmers of Infinite Wonder

In a galaxy far away, oh dear,
Aliens juggle planets with cheer.
They sneeze at the sun, it's a cosmic joke,
And laugh as the comets go up in smoke.

Stars wink at each other, quick and bright,
While meteors race in a comedic flight.
One slips and trips on a cosmic vine,
Yelling, "Oops! Can you pass the wine?"

Black holes gather dust, quite the mess,
As quirky quasars wear polka dot dress.
It's party time in the cosmic mall,
Where time and space just laugh and sprawl.

So grab your telescope, peep and see,
The giggles of the universe, wild and free.
With every twinkle, the laughter extends,
In endless wonder, where joy never ends.

A Dance of Cosmic Shadows

The shadows sway to a starlit tune,
With stars in tutus, dancing at noon.
Black holes spin silly, in a wobbly style,
While asteroids groove, making us smile.

Nebulae puff clouds of pink cotton candy,
And meteors tango, all dressed up dandy.
Planets do the cha-cha, so full of grace,
While comets play tag in a lively space.

Saturn throws rings in a playful toss,
As Uranus rolls back, just like a boss.
The moon's on a pogo stick, bouncing so high,
While Venus brings snacks, oh my, oh my!

In this cosmic disco, the vibe's outta sight,
Join in the fun under stars shining bright.
The universe giggles, a lighthearted scene,
As shadows dance wildly in the cosmic machine.

The Poetry of Celestial Bodies

Mars wrote a sonnet, but left out a rhyme,
While Jupiter claims it's always prime time.
Venus prefers haikus, short and sweet,
And Mercury's verses are quick on their feet.

The sun pens limericks that sparkle and glow,
And Neptune writes sonnets, oh so slow.
Pluto's a joker, cracking up the crowd,
With tales of his travels, funny and loud.

Asteroids send postcards from the deep dark,
Of cosmic adventures, what a wild lark!
While comets scribble notes on the breeze,
Whispering secrets among the stars and trees.

Celestial bodies share laughs in a line,
Their poetry dances, oh how it does shine!
In the vastness of night, where ideas take flight,
They compose a grand symphony, pure delight.

Echoes from the Astral Sea

In the waves of the cosmos, echoes arise,
Mermaids on asteroids wear sparkling ties.
They surf on starlight, giggling with glee,
Sipping stardust cocktails, fancy and free.

Galactic fish swim in a vibrant hue,
As they tell tales of planets they flew.
One caught a comet with a wink and a grin,
And danced through the nebulae, drawn in a spin.

The tides of the moons bring stories to tell,
Of cosmic capers where mischief does dwell.
Shooting stars sprinkle laughter like cheer,
As echoes of joy resonate far and near.

So listen closely to the whispers of night,
In the astral sea where laughter takes flight.
For in every ripple, a chuckle is rolled,
Tales of the universe, forever retold.

www.ingramcontent.com/pod-product-compliance
Lightning Source LLC
Chambersburg PA
CBHW051651160426
43209CB00004B/874